EXPLORERS WANTED!

In the Himalayas

Simon Chapman

EXPLORERS WANTED!

books by Simon Chapman

Simon Chapman
EXPLORERS
WANTED!

In the Himalayas

LITTLE, BROWN AND COMPANY

New York ❧ Boston

Little, Brown and Company

Time Warner Book Group
1271 Avenue of the Americas, New York, NY 10020
Visit our Web site at www.lb-kids.com

First U.S. Edition: September 2005

First published in Great Britain by Egmont Books Limited in 2004

Library of Congress Cataloging-in-Publication Data

Chapman, Simon.
    In the Himalayas/by Simon Chapman. — 1st U.S. ed.
        p. cm. — (Explorers wanted!)
    "First published in Great Britain by Edmont Books Limited in 2004" — T.p. verso.
    ISBN 0-316-15544-6
    1. Mountaineering — Himalaya mountains — Juvenile literature. 2. Himalaya
Mountains — Description and travel — Juvenile literature. I. Title.

    GV199.44.H55C48 2005
    796.522'095496 — dc22   2004061638

10 9 8 7 6 5 4 3 2 1

COM-MO

Printed in the United States of America

CONTENTS

SO...YOU WANT TO BE A HIMALAYAS EXPLORER?

You want to...

scale Dangiroba peak at the **"roof of the world"**?

search for **snow leopards, yaks, and yetis**?

brave the most **fearsome mountain range on the planet?**

If the answer to any of these questions is **YES**, then this is the book for you, so read on...

This book will give you the lowdown on how to mount an expedition into the high Himalayas, from trekking through lush, forested valleys and over rocky passes to braving avalanches and crevasses as you climb through the snow to an untouched mountain peak. Along the way, you'll find out about some of the people who came before you, some who succeeded . . . and others who tried but failed.

YOUR MISSION, should you choose to accept it, is to be the first person to climb "Dangiroba." It's not the highest peak or even the hardest to climb, but, like many summits, until now it has just been too out-of-the-way and difficult to get to. There are no roads within easy reach and trekking on foot is the only option. Just getting there will be an adventure. There'll be rivers to cross, perilous cliff-edge trails to traverse, and then there are the dark, creepy forests, rumored home of the legendary beast-man, the yeti. Does it really exist? Maybe you'll be the one to find out!

You'll have to cross the infamous Lohtang Pass and enter the isolated valley of Polpo, where the people herd yaks and drink their tea mixed with yak butter.

Finally, you'll attempt your ascent of "Dangiroba," climbing ice and rock so high up that you'll be gasping for breath at every step in the thin air. Watching out for avalanches that can sweep you away, you'll have to cross crevasse-strewn snowfields and then climb to the summit. It will be an adventure at the edge of human capabilities. Do you think you're up to the challenge?

Time to set the scene...

Himalayas means "Place of Snow" in the ancient Indian Sanskrit language. The "Roof of the World," as it has also been called, is vast.

The mountains range from Pakistan in the west right across the top of India, Nepal, and parts of China. There's more than just snow-capped summits. On the southern side, foothills that are fair-sized mountains in their own right steadily rise up to famous high Himalayan peaks like Everest, K2, and Annapurna, which you may have heard of before. Beyond those giants, only slightly lower in altitude, lies the cold plateau of Tibet.

What you find in the Himalayas depends on how high up you are and how much rain (or snow) the place receives. As you climb through the foothills, you'll pass through rhododendron forests and high alpine pastures where yaks and goats graze, and cold, barren deserts in the "rain shadow" of the peaks. Going up still further, you'll come to the bare rock and ice fields of the summits themselves.

The Andes mountain chain in South America is almost as high as the Himalayas and many of the animals are similar.

Andes — viscacha, vicuna, spectacled bear.

Himalayas — marmot, chiru antelope, Himalayan black bear.

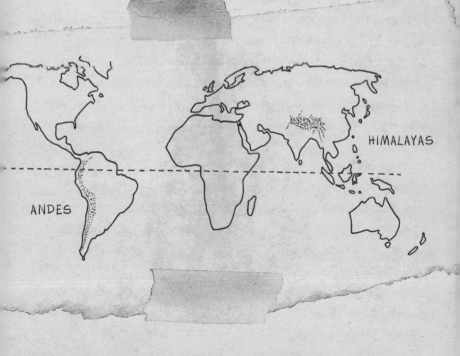

HIMALAYAS

ANDES

Chapter 1
TO THE SNOWS OF DANGIROBA

The time of year when you are traveling is the short season between the summer monsoon rains and the autumn, when the high passes become blocked with snow. When the sun is out it can feel like you're frying in the tropical heat, but as soon as a cloud passes or you enter the shade of a narrow ravine, you'll be struck by the sudden cold, especially when you cross the wild, icy torrents of melted water that gush down the valleys.

High up on the sides of an enormous valley, the vegetation is low and wind-blasted. Small bushes cling to cracks and fissures in the rocks, hugging the ground to avoid being uprooted. The slope is steep and sheer in places. The trail you've been trudging all morning zigzags up and out of sight. At the head of the valley, peaks of bare rock and dazzling white snow rise up on either side. The slightly lower saddle-shaped gap in between is the Lohtang Pass, which you will have to cross on your journey to get to the gleaming white pyramid of "Dangiroba," which pokes above the clouds in the far distance.

There is some movement on the trail ahead. Silhouetted against the sky, something huge and shaggy is approaching, lumbering slowly toward you. Your mind races through the possibilities.

A Himalayan brown bear — easily able to run you down?
A snow leopard — elusive and so well camouflaged that it's nearly invisible among the rocks and snow of its high mountain habitat?
A yeti — legendary hairy ape-man of the Himalayas, rumored to be dangerous?

SNOW LEOPARD

YETI

HIMALAYAN BROWN BEAR

7

The brown bear – leopard – yeti is getting closer. You can now make out two spindly human legs beneath the shambling mound. "Namaste," the woman says to you from beneath her heavy load of hay as she passes and continues back toward her village.

You continue up the path. With each step, you are forced to pause for breath. Your head feels dizzy and it feels as though iced water has been poured inside the veins of your legs. How did you get so out of shape? It's the altitude. This high up, the air is so thin that you're struggling to take in enough oxygen with each breath. How do the locals

do it? How did that little woman manage with a whole haystack on her back when you can barely manage with nothing to carry? The answer is that she lives here, and you would be just as fit if you did too. You need to spend time in the high mountain air. You need to acclimatize. . . .

Chapter 2
GETTING YOUR ACT TOGETHER
(Altitude: 2,000 meters)

Acclimatizing means getting your body used to living at a high altitude, where the air is thin and your body has to work harder to get the oxygen it needs. Red blood cells carry oxygen to your muscles to help them work. The air high in the mountains is at a lower pressure and so it's more spread out. When you spend time here your body makes more red blood cells to get around the problem. The result is that within a week or so you become acclimatized and no longer have difficulty walking, running, and doing exercise. Incidentally, if you then go down to sea level you feel super-fit for a while with all those extra red cells carrying the oxygen around. That's why many athletes like to train in places that are high above sea level.

You've decided to acclimatize at Darpeeling, a hill town where many years ago rich people used to come and have their holidays away from the stifling heat of the lowlands. Darpeeling is 2,000 meters above sea level with cool fresh air, blue skies, and a view in the distance of the snowy peak of "Dangiroba."

Darpeeling is the last town of any size where you can buy food, organize a guide, and perhaps hire some porters as well as a truck to take you to where the road ends in the Gali Kandaki Valley. It is here that you will organize your expedition.

There are several trekking agencies that equip would-be adventurers, and at one of these you meet up with Da-Lhamhu, a Sherpani (lady Sherpa), who is going to guide you on your trek as well as carry some of the gear. The Sherpas are a tribe of people who live in just a few valleys in the high Himalayas of Nepal. Over the years, they have earned a reputation for being the best guides and porters for Himalayan expeditions. More Sherpas than any other nationality have climbed Earth's highest peak, Mount Everest. Sherpa Tenzing Norgay was one of the first two men to get to the summit in 1953 (the other was Edmund Hillary, a New Zealander). Apa Sherpa climbed the mountain twelve times. Babu Chhiri

Sherpa bivouacked on the summit for twenty-one hours. He also set the record for the fastest ascent. Da-Lhamhu hasn't been on that many expeditions; but having been raised in the mountains, she should be able to assist you, translate the local language, and get your expedition equipped for the journey ahead.

Getting equipped

You're going to need equipment for all levels in the mountains. First, you'll have to carry basic trekking equipment like sturdy boots, a tent, and cooking gear. Then, when you make your actual ascent of "Dangiroba," you'll need some highly specialized gear like crampons, ice axes, and oxygen tanks. All this climbing equipment will only be useful for your attempt at the summit. For the rest of your expedition, it will be useless deadweight that somebody will have to carry. To get to the remote monastery of Thamap, where the real climbing begins, you have a long and arduous journey ahead of you. You'll have to organize how you will transport all this equipment the entire way since there are no transportation-friendly roads where you're going.

WATERPROOF COAT AND OVER-PANTS MADE FROM BREATHABLE FABRIC THAT WILL LET MOISTURE (CONDENSATION AND SWEAT) OUT.

This means you're going to need human porters or animals to carry it all. You can hire both at villages along the way though they're not likely to want to travel beyond the next village, at which point you'll need to get more carriers.

- Light, easy-to-dry clothing.
- Other useful items: A walking stick or trekking poles.
- Specialized mountain gear for you and Da-Lhamhu. That stuff will stay sealed in two knapsacks that are not to be opened until the real climbing starts (we'll look at it in more detail in chapter seven).

Da-Lhamhu says you can buy most of your food supplies here at Darpeeling. You'll also be able to buy more provisions at villages along your route, but you can't depend on that.

By the end of your shopping spree, you have eight sacks of lentils, rice, and other dry, easy-to-carry food, not to mention your knapsacks of mountain-climbing gear.

KNAPSACK

HIKING
BOOTS

TREKKING
POLE

Planning your route: Quiz

This is a map of your planned route to "Dangiroba," with the altitude marked in meters. You'll be traveling from some fairly low-level jungles right up to the high summits, where the temperatures rarely get above freezing. Look at the map and answer the questions ...

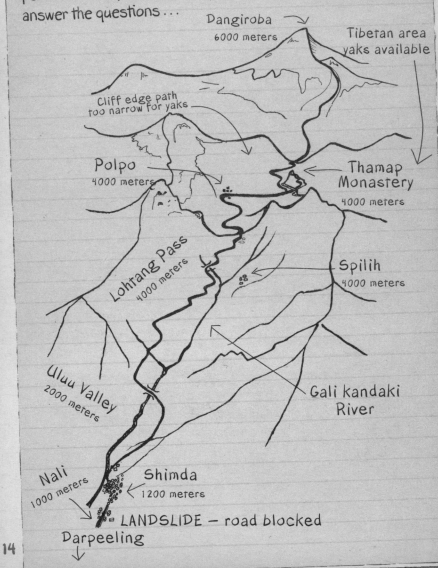

Dangiroba
6000 meters

Tibetan area
yaks available

Cliff edge path
too narrow for yaks

Polpo
4000 meters

Thamap
Monastery
4000 meters

Lohtang Pass
4000 meters

Spilih
4000 meters

Gali kandaki
River

Uluu Valley
2000 meters

Nali
1000 meters

Shimda
1200 meters

LANDSLIDE — road blocked

Darpeeling

1. Which is the farthest village you'll be able to get to by truck?
2. Where will you have to wade across a river?
3. From which point will you need cold weather clothing?
4. At which settlements might you be able to buy food?
5. Which is the only village where it is worthwhile hiring pack yaks to carry your equipment?
6. At which village, Nali or Polpo, will you probably have to pay any villagers you hire as porters more money for their services?
7. Can you think why at Polpo you could manage with fewer porters than at Nali?
8. Which settlement might be a safe place to leave your food supplies for the return journey?

Answers on page 16

By the end of the week, you are already feeling fitter in the mountain air and all your provisions have been bought. Da-Lhamhu has gone ahead to the last village on the road, Nali, to hire porters. With the climbing permits sorted, you are now ready to follow with the sacks of food and knapsacks of mountain equipment — a truckload of stuff driven by Gupta Bedi, or "King of the mountain roads," as he likes to call himself.

Decorated with paintings of many-armed gods, tigers, and multi-colored swirling designs, Gupta's truck is quite a

sight. He drives it very fast, beeping his horn at everything, it seems — at friends who wave, cows, chickens . . . even monkeys in the road. Most of all he sounds the horn at any other driver who dares to share the road with him. The mountain roads are narrow and winding, often with steep cliffs above and below. Meeting oncoming traffic inevitably means that someone has to give way — usually at the last minute. It's terrifying for whoever is on the outside of the bend — and worse where the road narrows to a single lane.

Answers from pages 14–15

1. Nali. The dirt road goes to Shimda, but a landslide has destroyed it.

2. Uluu Valley.

3. Around the Lohtang Pass.

4. Nali, Shimda, and Polpo. Thamap is a monastery, so it won't have food to sell. Spilih isn't on your route and, besides, it is too small to have surplus food to sell you.

5. Polpo. You could hire yaks at Thamap, but they would not be able to manage the difficult terrain up to base camp.

6. Nali. Any porters hired here would have to travel at least three days before reaching the next village, Polpo, crossing the cold, high Lohtang Pass on the way.

7. By the time you get there you will have eaten your way through some of your provisions and not have as much to carry.

8. Thamap — at the monastery (first choice) or Polpo (second choice). You can't really risk leaving it outside. People might find it, or bears or wolves might eat it!

hen Gupta and the driver
acing him seem to charge
t each other, horns
onking, seeing who will
hicken out first. It's
usually the driver on the
downhill side who gives
n. The truck crunches
nto reverse and then
backs up until the tail-
gate is right over some
sheer drop. The other
ruck squeezes
past with only
centimeters to
spare. The drivers
briefly wind their windows
down, have a quick conversation,
there's more horn-honking, and then
they're off again. In places you see
scars of broken vegetation and bare soil
andslides at the edges. Far below there are bits
of truck wreckage. No wonder people put up signs like these ...

Horn Please! (Let me know you're coming round that
blind corner!)

Lane Driving is Sane Driving. (Don't drive on the
wrong side of the road.)

Danger Begins Where Safety Ends.

Chapter 3
PLANT HUNTERS AND DEER WITH FANGS

By the time Gupta brings the truck to a halt at the village of Nali, late in the afternoon, you're feeling exhilarated but also rather relieved to have made it this far.

JANGBU

ANG

BABU

Da-Lhamhu has organized some porters for you. Ang, Babu, and Jangbu will help carry your food and gear up the Gali Kandaki Valley over the Lohtang Pass to the village of Polpo. The three are all very strong and very eager, according to Da-Lhamhu. You're not all that convinced by her confidence.

Note that although each of your porters is carrying the same mass — around 32 kg — the loads aren't very evenly distributed. Can you think why? Answer the questions on the following page.

The loads are . . .

Ang

water bag	6 kg
dried food — rice, pasta, oats, etc.	23 kg
personal belongings	3 kg

Babu

your tent, roll mat, and sleeping bag	6 kg
ropes, harnesses, and climbing gear	10 kg
oxygen tanks	6 kg
personal belongings and porters' tent	6 kg
porters' food	6 kg

Jangbu

sack of potatoes	12 kg
small sack of onions	6 kg
bag of lentils	6 kg
bag of turnips	4 kg
personal belongings	4 kg

Meanwhile, what are you carrying? Cold/wet-weather clothing, a torch, medical kit, some food, spare clothing, and trainers — total mass 15 kg. This is nothing like the mass carried by your porters, but it certainly feels heavy enough, especially considering those steep mountains you're climbing. What about Da-Lhamhu, your Sherpina? She's carrying around 30 kg like the porters — food mainly, but also some ropes and climbing gear such as the crampons and two ice axes.

1. Whose food should you eat first — Ang's, Babu's, or Jangbu's? Can you think why this would make this man the luckiest porter?

2. Whose load will hardly change during the trek?

3. Which gear should you be carrying for your own safety?

4. Which part of Ang's load could be reduced to nothing for most of the day in the low-level (but not frozen) parts of the trek?

5. Who should be most careful when crossing rivers so that his load does not become waterlogged?

6. Which of the men are you counting on as being trustworthy?

7. Along the trail, you'll see the porters picking up any sticks or brushwood they find — why is that?

Answers on page 27

The village of Nali is at a lower altitude than Darpeeling. You're well acclimatized and actually feel quite strong at the moment. Not that the route is easy. You skirt the valley sides, steadily winding higher, first past terraced fields and then rough pasture where sheep and cows graze. You can see other small settlements below, but as the day wears on these become fewer, spaced between areas of scrub and woods of birch and pine trees. Higher still, you come across rhododendrons, the same shiny-leaved bushes with the purple or pink flowers that you come across in many parks and gardens at home. In fact, many of the plants, especially the flowers you see here, look familiar. Here's why . . .

Joseph Hooker and the Plant Hunters

His expedition to the kingdom of Sikkim in 1848 was the largest of its kind. There were fifty-six people, ranging from porters to red-coated Nepali guards armed with swords and Gurkha-curved kukri knives. There were boys trained to climb trees and gather orchids and even a taxidermist to stuff any new species of bird or animal that they discovered and shot along the way.

Hooker explored from the tropical valleys right up to the snowy passes and slopes of "Kanchenjunga" (the sixth-highest mountain in the world). At one high ridge above the snow line, he experienced the strange "Spirit of Brocken" phenomenon when he saw his enormous shadow cast by the sun behind him, complete with a halo, projected onto the mist below. He climbed higher than any other European explorer had at the time, even though he had no specialist equipment and had to improvise on things like snow goggles. (His were made from a woman's veil tied around his eyes.) Even his tent couldn't have been that good. Since zippers hadn't been invented, the front flap was merely tied across and on several occasions, Hooker was woken up during the night by inquisitive yaks poking their heads through the opening and breathing on him.

It wasn't the forbidding terrain, wildlife, or hostile weather conditions that caused this great gardener-explorer the greatest problems, however. It was the rulers of the valleys he traveled through. They thought, What on Earth was this Englishman with his enormous retinue of servants and porters up to? Why would anyone want to climb the highest, coldest, most inhospitable mountains unless he was an agent of the British Empire sent to seize our land? The rajahs had bridges destroyed and forbade villagers to sell food to Hooker's expedition. They set out false border markers. One local king even held Hooker and his companion, Campbell (it was his wife who had provided the veil for the snow goggles), captive for a couple of months. All of this was for some flowers for a garden in far-off England!

RHODODENDRON

These forests of rhododendrons and pine trees may seem just like those at home, but don't kid yourself. These are much wilder.

Here are some of the animals that live here …

Musk deer

A deer with fangs! It has been hunted remorselessly for the musk gland that lies beneath the abdomen skin of the males. This gives out a scent that females find attractive but to humans smells like stale urine. However, when dried it's supposed to smell so nice that for years people have used it as the base for perfumes. (Con men sometimes try to sell tourists the glands from goats' necks, saying they're musk deer glands. They rub the gland on one side of your hand while sneakily smearing perfume on the other side so it seems that the smell has the power to go right through.)

Red panda

Looks cute and cuddly, rather like an orange, badger-sized teddy bear with a bushy tail. They forage for fruit and grubs mainly at night and are unusual because the underside of their paws is covered in fur, making them useless for gripping, which seems a bit strange in a tree-climbing animal. Red pandas give out a nasty stink from a gland near their bottom when they get excited, so this is an animal that's best seen but not approached too closely.

Himalayan black bear

(Sometimes called the moon bear because of the white crescent-shaped mark on its chest). They're not the biggest of bears, at only one and a half meters tall (the brown bears that live above the tree line are huge by comparison), but they are another creature not to approach too closely. They wouldn't want to eat you, but they are rather partial to corn cobs and apricots, both of which are grown as crops by the hill farmers around here. Black bears get particularly angry when caught by surprise or when someone tries to stop them from eating his fruit. This is a bear with a truly murderous rage. There are many cases of villagers being killed by apricot-eating bears throwing a tantrum after being caught munching in their fruit trees.

Takin

A strange herbivore that's related to goats and antelopes, but is not quite either. With the face of a wildebeest and short, strong, sturdy legs, it lives on the steepest, most thickly forested slopes in the bamboo and rhododendron jungle. Occasionally takins get together in herds of 300 or more.

Answers from page 20

1. Jangbu. Potatoes are heavy and bulky. Of course, eating them would give Jangbu far less to carry.

2. Babu's.

3. The bag containing your roll mat, a tent, and sleeping bag.

4. The water bag — he can refill it at any mountain stream or river.

5. Ang. The dried food soaks up water easily and would then spoil unless eaten quickly.

6. Babu. He's carrying the most valuable equipment.

7. They'll use it as firewood!

That night, you make camp on a flat, grassy area at the opening of a narrow, thickly forested valley. Tomorrow, Da-Lhamhu says, you will skirt around the valley a short way, cross the river that cuts through it, and from there it's a two-day trek over the pass to Polpo. Exhausted, you retreat to your tent and huddle in your sleeping bag. Outside you can hear the chuckle of the porters and Da-Lhamhu exchanging jokes around a crackling fire . . . and rather ominously you can hear the rumble of distant thunder.

Chapter 4
RAGING RIVERS AND THE FILTHY SNOWMAN

It rained during the night and your grassy ledge is sodden. A cloying mist hangs over the valley. You can scarcely see more than a hundred meters in any direction. The mossy branches of the gnarled mountain trees ahead look slightly menacing in the gloom, and the three porters are sullen and grumpy as you break camp and start walking. The plastic sheet they had been using as a tent blew over in the night. Now, feeling damp and in low spirits, they take their time eating the *tsampa*, "ground barley porridge," that Da-Lhamhu boils up for breakfast. She says you should be able to get to a good camping spot near the Lohtang Pass today, but only if you set off early and make good time. Da-Lhamhu tries to badger everyone along to set off. It's obvious she's worried about something.

You soon realize what she's so anxious about. With the rain during the night, even the smallest streams have turned into raging torrents. What about the river that carved out this ravine? How much has it grown with the extra water?

Soon your worst fears are realized. The path has been going downhill for a while and the roar of rushing water gets steadily louder. Now you begin to get some idea of just how much force a river can have. The entire surface is white with frothy waves. The river pelts down the gully, surging up past house-sized boulders. You can hear grinding as rocks slide against each other in the current. There might have been a bridge here, judging from the fact that the path carries on across the other side. Maybe the bridge was swept away as the water rose during the night. All that remains now is a log that spans the gap

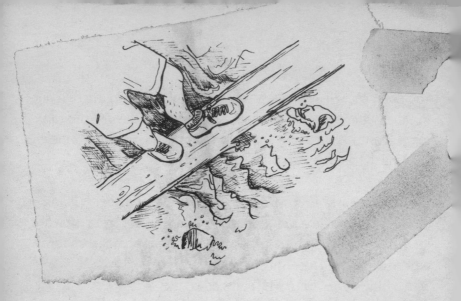

between the rocky bank on your side and some boulders in the middle. You notice with dismay that even if you get across the log, you'll then have to wade across the other half of the river.

You summon up the willpower to step on the log and start to shuffle across, a bit like a tightrope walker. You can see the water racing by underneath. It has an almost hypnotic effect. You know you have to concentrate on your footing and getting to the other side. Out of the corner of your eye, you can see Jangbu following close behind you. He doesn't even bother to look down. He's done river crossings like this many times before. His face looks calm and his eyes are fixed on the rocks ahead as he steadily walks across the log.

Now the difficult part. If there was a log across here, it's now been washed away. There is no alternative but to wade across.

How to cross a raging river

Here's how you can do it — if you dare. Use your ropes. You need to get a line across the water that can help all the porters across.

It is unlikely that anyone else in your team can swim. That means you'll have to be the one to cross first. This might be easiest without your pack. Maybe you'll be able to rig up some rope-pulley system to ferry it across above the river. What about your boots? Should you take them off? If you soak them, they'll take ages — possibly days — to dry, and as you will soon be climbing above the snow line this could mean freezing your boots solid and possibly risking frostbite of your toes. Barefoot then? You would save your boots, but you could stub your toes or hurt your feet. Surprisingly, bare feet don't grip that well — not as well as socks. If you cross a stony river, you have better grip if you keep your socks on.

Shipton's Close Shave

In 1931, the British climber Eric Shipton, climbing the Himalayan mountain "Nanda Devi," had just this problem. He had spotted a cave in a cliff on the other side of a fast-flowing river where he figured his party could rest for the night before continuing up the river gorge. He tied the end of a rope to his waist and waded in, using the end of his ice-ax to probe the way. The river was swollen and icy cold with freshly melted snow. The waist-high water whirled him round, but he kept his footing even though his feet were going numb. Stones, washed with the current, bashed and cut his legs. Once he was across, his climbing partner, Tilman, and then two of the porters, Pasang and Angtharkay, started across. They were heavily laden down and much shorter than Shipton. What's more, they couldn't swim. The water, which had been waist-high to the Englishman, was up to Angtharkay's chest. He was carrying a huge load of bedding and clothing, which became soaked and started to pull him down. He slipped, going in up to his neck, but luckily kept hold of the rope. In the nick of time, Pasang, who was also carrying a heavy load, grabbed his arm and saved him.

River crossing — Quiz

1. What can you use to help keep your balance? (Look at your equipment list in chapter two.)

2. What other piece of your climbing gear should you keep attached to you?

3. Which way should you face — upstream, downstream, or in the direction you're crossing?

4. If you fall, you should make sure your feet are pointing which way — upstream, downstream, or sideways into the current?

5. Should the next person behind you start across before you have made it to the other side?

6. What should you do with the piece of gear that you gave as the answer to question two when you've made it across?

Answers on page 34

Oh! Oh! Oh! That's cold! The shock of plunging into such icy water (some of it's melted from glaciers higher up the mountain) momentarily knocks the wind out of you and in getting a grip on the slippery rocks, you soon soak yourself.

The next part's tricky. You edge sideways across the flow, using the stick for support. The water is thigh-high — any higher and you're sure it would pull you over. It's getting shallower now . . . you're there. There's no obvious fixing point, like a tree, to tie the rope onto, so you brace yourself as Jangbu comes across.

Your expedition gets across the river without incident and you carry on for a while until you reach another swollen torrent you need to cross in the next valley.

Answers from page 33

1. A walking stick/trekking pole.
2. A rope. Stay roped up because if you fall, the others should be able to pull you back to shore.
3. Upstream, so you can lean into the current.
4. Downstream, so you can fend off rocks rather than hitting them head first.
5. No.
6. Tie your rope to something secure, ready for the next person to cross. If you can't tie it onto something, keep hold of the rope and brace yourself just in case she falls.

This time the stream is narrower but deeper, and it's too risky to try wading across. Da-Lhamhu suggests trying another path she spotted a little way back. The trail veers off up the valley, following the river's course upstream, and eventually crosses it at a point where it gushes between two large boulders. They're just close enough together that you can jump across. You're so busy congratulating yourselves for being skillful that you hardly notice when Jangbu quietly points out that you are lost. You're in some narrow sub-valley that none of the porters nor Da-Lhamhu has ever entered before. It's shady and cool. High rock

walls block the sunlight out. Your porters are grumbling. They say you should be back on the main trail by now and that this shortcut has made you lost. What's more, they are scared that "something" is out there.

Everyone hurries to get back to the main path. Despite the fact that the porters are carrying twice your load, they and Da-Lhamhu soon leave you behind, daydreaming about a bird you glimpsed briefly just a short way back. It was dull, gray-green, and dumpy looking, like some sort of

MONAL
PHEASANT

pheasant — nothing to write home about until it caught the sunlight and suddenly lit up metallic orange and green: a Monal pheasant. The shimmering colors are caused by the transparent feather filaments scattering the light into the colors of the rainbow — red, orange, yellow, green, blue, indigo, violet — then reflecting back only one or two colors.

A rustling of leaves to your side startles you into alertness. You spin around and catch a glimpse of shaggy red-brown fur disappearing into the tangle of rhododendrons.
A bear? *No, it's the wrong color.*
A red panda? *No, it's too large.*
A takin? *No, you were sure this animal was on two feet, not four.*
A yeti?

With your mind spinning, you hurry on after the porters . . .

Yeti Facts

In 1951, Eric Shipton came across a line of tracks in the snow on the Menlung Glacier, close to Mount Everest. The footprints were fifty centimeters long by thirty-five centimeters wide. They were obviously made by something with a long stride walking on two, not four, feet. "Yeti," the Sherpa guides announced. The climbers followed the trail for a mile before it disappeared on hard ice.

Of course, the people of the Himalayan valleys have known about yetis for generations. It was one of their names, Metohkangmi or "filthy snowman," which was mistranslated into "abominable snowman" by European travelers. To the mountain people, yetis are just another type of animal like snow leopards or Bharal blue sheep. They even have paintings of them in some of their Buddhist monasteries.

Stories have been told of yetis killing villagers' yaks or making off with women and children, but yetis are hardly ever seen, let alone encountered at close range. Reinhold Mess-

ner, the Italian mountaineer who was the first person to climb Everest without oxygen tanks, claimed to have seen yetis four times. The closest he came to one (in 1986) was about twenty meters. It was asleep but soon woke up and stared at Messner before ambling away. Another time he saw a two-meter-tall, shaggy, black-haired yeti along with a smaller red-haired one. Messner thought these two were a mother and child. However, Messner has since gone back on his claims, saying that the yeti is really just the little-known Tibetan blue bear.

Fact or fiction?

Here is some yeti information. You decide ...

- There are said to be two types of yeti. One is around two meters tall, with long black-gray or dark brown hair. The other kind is much smaller and has red-brown hair. It has been said that young yetis lose their red hair as they grow up.
- Some people have said that the yeti may be a type of "Gigantopithecus," an extinct type of early man that died out two million years ago.

GIGANTOPITHECUS

- The yeti could be a bear. The Tibetan blue bear is so rare that it is only known from a couple of skins and a few bones.
- Bears can walk on two feet for short distances.
- It is said that when Tibetan blue bears walk through deep snow they put their hind feet into the prints of their forepaws. This makes the going easier and also makes the tracks look like they've been made by something walking on two feet.
- Before the Second World War, the Nazis sent a scientist to check out the facts. The scientist came back with two blue bears (he told Reinhold Messner) but no giant ape.
- Every time scientists have analyzed "supposed" yeti skins, they've turned out to belong to bears or mountain goats.
- Yetis most likely live in the rhododendron forests, where food would be easier to find than in the high snow fields. There are still plenty of remote valleys where yetis could live undisturbed.
- In 2001, members of a British expedition to Bhutan were taken to the hollow base of a cedar tree where a yeti was said to have recently slept the night. Four hair samples were taken. When DNA from these samples was analyzed, it was found not

to match the DNA of any animal currently known to science. You hurry on, not catching up with the others on the main trail until late afternoon, when the sun has gone down over the western ridges. Though it's not dark yet, everything is cloaked in lengthening shadows, and keeping your footing on the rocky path is becoming difficult. The porters are grumbling again. Why carry on to the stream where Da-Lhamhu wants to make tonight's camp, they point out, when there's a good campsite just a short way back?

Decide where you should make camp tonight — Quiz

This picture shows the two places where you could set up your tents, and opposite are the arguments for and against the campsites...

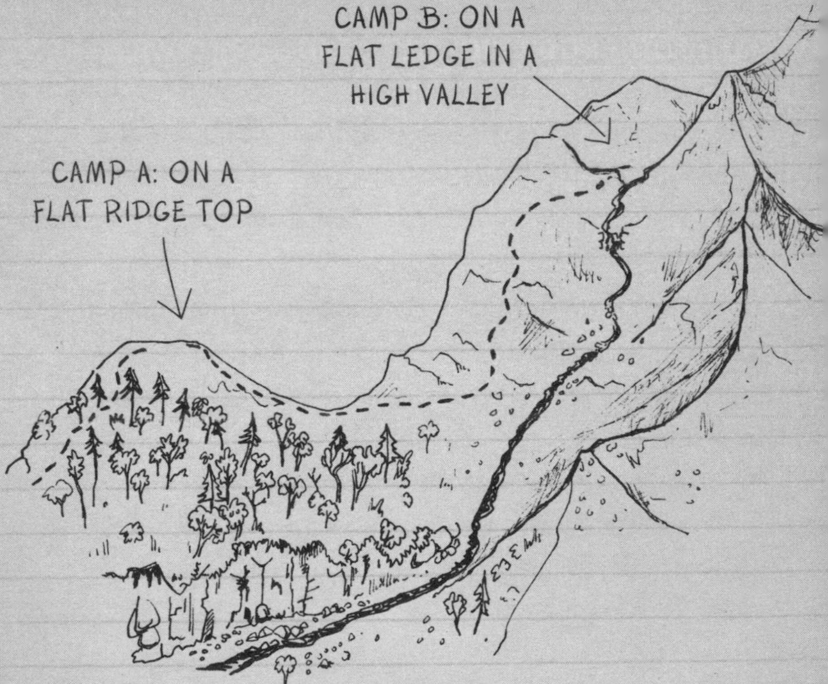

CAMP B: ON A FLAT LEDGE IN A HIGH VALLEY

CAMP A: ON A FLAT RIDGE TOP

1. Exposed position — cold and windy.
2. Stream nearby — easy access to water.
3. Steep uphill walk to reach it.
4. Lots of trees for firewood.
5. Little firewood nearby.
6. In a sheltered valley.
7. No water nearby.
8. Just a short walk back.

Which four arguments will your porters use to say you should go back to Camp A?
(Find two arguments for Camp A and two arguments against Camp B.)

Which four arguments will Da-Lhamhu use to persuade them to carry on to Camp B?
(Find two arguments for Camp B and two arguments against Camp A.)

Answers on page 42

Of course, the main reason for going on is so you will be closer to the Lohtang Pass. It's a hard day's hike over to the next valley and the village of Polpo. It's cold and exposed up on the pass and there are no good places to camp, so it would make more sense to get as close as possible before you start that trek. However, all this discussion has taken up valuable time. It's clearly getting too dark to carry on. Tonight you will have to camp at A.

As the gray twilight dims into night, the five of you pick your way back down the trail to the open ridge to make your last camp before your attempt on the Lohtang Pass.

Chapter 5
SMASHING BONES AT THE LOHTANG PASS

The cold wakes you up. You check your watch — it's four in the morning. Peering outside your tent, you see a glitter of frost over the ground and on the plastic tarpaulin that your porters have covered themselves with. You zip up the tent's front flap and snuggle down into your sleeping bag, curling yourself up into a ball to conserve heat. No matter how you position yourself, there's always some part of you that feels the chill. Sleep eludes you, and you hear the scrunch of soft footfalls outside. One of the porters? No, these are too quiet, too well practiced at stealth. As silently as you can manage, you start to slide the tent flap open. Whatever is outside is still there. Z-z-zip! The flap is open now. The footfalls are moving away. You stick your head out of the tent just in time to glimpse a low, light-colored cat form — perhaps it had spots; it was hard to tell. Whatever it was bounds down the slope into the blackness. There are tracks in the frost: four clawless toes and a central pad.

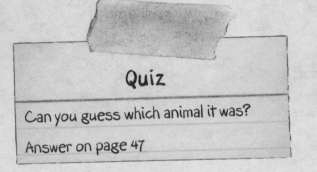

Quiz

Can you guess which animal it was?

Answer on page 47

Unable to sleep now, you pull on your boots and coat (you had been sleeping in the rest of your clothes since it was so cold) and try to revive the embers of last night's campfire. A lot of blowing and a few scrunched-up balls of dry toilet paper eventually do the trick. You get a small flame and start adding brushwood until the fire is strong enough to boil a pan of water, enough for some tea and to make some of the "tsampa" barley porridge that everyone eats to keep themselves going around here. Then you wait for the others to get up.

Quiz

Ugh! The tea's only lukewarm even though it was bubbling furiously when you poured it. Can you think why the tea is less than 100 degrees Celsius?

A. The freezing air has cooled the water down between boiling and pouring.

B. Something in the Himalayan water makes it boil at a lower temperature.

C. Water boils at a lower temperature at high altitude.

Answer on page 47

11:00 a.m.

Trekking onwards and upwards. When will all this uphill end? You've been trudging steadily upwards, zigzagging back and forth all morning. You ended up drinking all that tea yourself. None of the others got up until after seven, and

your porters weren't exactly eager about breaking camp and setting off again. The more you and Da-Lhamhu tried to urge them to hurry up, the more they seemed to slow down.

Da-Lhamhu says you must get over the Lohtang Pass today, and the earlier the better. There are no more good places to camp until beyond the pass, and if the weather gets bad, it would be unpleasant staying up there. She pretends to shiver. You get the idea. You must get to Polpo village tonight — that's the plan.

2:00 p.m.

The Lohtang Pass is at the head of the valley, a low dip of open ground between snow-covered peaks. By now you're far above the tree line. Here there are just grassy tussocks and a few scattered ground-hugging bushes between the stones and bare rock. From time to time you see mar-mots, rabbit-sized rodents that dash down into their burrows as you come close. High on the mountain slopes to the sides of the pass you make out the forms of some sort of **bearded** mountain goat. A pair of them seem to be trying to head-butt each other. One leaps down the rocks to attack its rival, keeping its footing on the virtually sheer slopes even after it has bounced off the other's **sickle-shaped** horns.

MARMOT

Answer from page 44

Snow leopard.

Answer from page 45

C. The higher up you are, the lower the air pressure and the easier it is for water to turn from liquid to gas. On top of Mount Everest (at 8,850 meters high) water boils at around 70 degrees Celsius compared to 100 degrees Celsius at sea level. Answer A is probably partly right as well.

"Markhor," says Da-Lhamhu. Reread the descriptions of the animals on the previous page and then use the key to find out if she was right.

Does it have a beard?
Are its horns curved or straight?
Does it have a ruff?

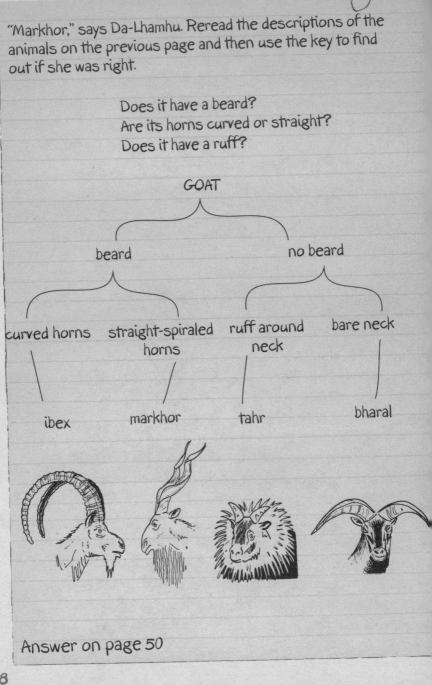

GOAT

beard — no beard

curved horns — straight-spiraled horns — ruff around neck — bare neck

ibex — markhor — tahr — bharal

Answer on page 50

48

You have little time to consider the niceties of mountain goat identification, however. Something comes hurtling down from the sky and shatters to pieces on a bare slab of rock right in front of you. A bone — a goat leg bone? — lands at your feet. Above, a large vulture hovers innocently on the up- drafts. Has it been bombing you with bones? You're inclined to think not until, a few minutes later, something similar happens again. You hear a clatter behind you and spin around to see the vulture swoop down to pick up the bone, hover high again, and then drop it back onto the rock slab you had been walking across. BINGO! This time the bone shat- ters. The bird lands, picks up a long shard of bone in its hooked beak, and, like a sword swallower, slides it down its throat.

Bone marrow — that's what it's after. If you're a lammergeier bearded vulture, you can forget skin and gristle and the usual slim pickings that other vultures and ravens go for. If you want a truly nutritious meal, you go straight for the marrow. But how to get at it? That's the problem.

Answer from page 48

Horns curved, no ruff, a beard. That was an ibex. Markhors are very similar but they have spiraled, not curved, horns.

How to get to the marrow (if you're a lammergeier)

1. Find yourself a mountain-goat carcass.
2. Pick out a leg bone. They contain the most marrow.
3. Take it to a great height above a large flat rock.
4. Drop bone.
5. Repeat steps three and four until it shatters (fifty to sixty times is fairly normal).
6. Fly down, pick up bone shards.
7. Swallow whole.

Stomach acid does the rest. A lammergeier's is so strong that even while the top end of the bone is still sticking out of the bird's mouth, the lower end is dissolving, ready to be digested.

Moving on up...

The path is becoming indistinct; there are now lots of paths where different groups of people have chosen their own way to go up. To mark the main route, someone has thoughtfully left piles of stones. Some of these "cairns" have sticks stuck in them with ragged white flags flapping in the wind. Da-Lhamhu explains that they are Buddhist prayer flags. Each flutter sends another prayer off to heaven.

Soon you realize you are no longer climbing. The ground is leveling off now; you are reaching the divide between the Gali Kandaki Valley and Polpo, which you are about to enter. In the clear mountain air, you can see your route ahead into the next valley and beyond in amazing detail. Polpo is a dry, desert-like, bowl-shaped dip. You can see terraced fields around a cluster of houses that are walled together almost like a small fort. Beyond, a narrow valley snakes up toward a great white triangle of snow and rock — "Dangiroba" — your destination.

Compared to the route you have taken so far with its forests and meadows, Polpo looks brown and barren. Why the sudden change? Why does the way ahead look so desolate?

Chapter 6
YAKETY-YAK

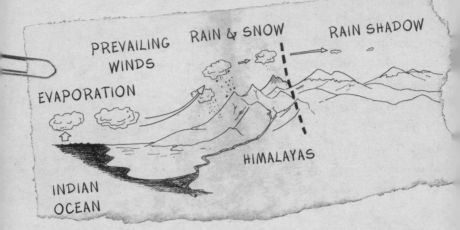

Rain shadow. That's the reason for Polpo's barrenness. By the time the winds from the Indian Ocean have reached that far into the mountains, they've already rained out nearly all of their moisture. Here's how it works . . .

Water is evaporated in the Indian Ocean and, at a certain height, the vapor cools and condenses into clouds of tiny droplets. Winds blow the clouds toward the mountains, and as the clouds rise up to get over them the clouds get cooler. The tiny water droplets collect together. Soon they are so heavy that they fall out of the sky as rain. If they are cold enough, they freeze into crystals and fall as snow. Most of this rain and snow falls on the first set of high mountains the clouds reach. These areas naturally have lush vegetation and raging rivers. Beyond, further into the Himalayas, the valleys and mountain slopes are much drier. Few clouds make it that far, so rain is infrequent. This effect is called the rain shadow.

Da-Lhamhu looks happier now. She can see that you will reach the walled settlement of Polpo by nightfall. You'll have a warmer night under a real roof. You'll be able to buy food rather than running your supplies down. You'll be able to pay off your porters and hire others to take you to the monastery of Thamap at the end of the winding valley, the last stage before your ascent of "Dangiroba." At a relaxed pace, you set off down the trail toward the village.

Appearances can be deceptive. Polpo may have looked close, but the terrain is still difficult. It's nearly nightfall by the time you arrive. Boys are herding goats and a few horses into the protection of the settlement's walls. The animals occupy the ground floor of the houses. Ladders lead up to floors above where the people live. There's a smell of dust and smoke around the place, but what is it they're burning? Apart from scraggy juniper bushes on the valley sides and a few trees around the village, there doesn't appear to be anything you could use as fuel. But look what that girl's carrying in her basket. Yak poop!

It was her job today to pick up the droppings of her dad's herd. It's not that bad ... they're fairly dry and after a few more days in the sun and wind they'll be as good as barbecue briquettes. They are clean-burning, a renewable resource (yaks are always going to keep pooping), and they're free!

Avoiding several very large, very fierce guard dogs that people have chained up to their houses, you make it into the village without mishap. Da-Lhamhu arranges for all of you (you, Da, and the three Nali porters) to sleep in an empty storehouse at the edge of town.

She also pays for half of a goat carcass for you to roast on this your last night with Ang, Babu, and Jangbu. Tomorrow they will set off for home after a little bit of "trade" they have planned. It's only now you find out that some of the weight they carried that you thought was personal

belongings was in fact goods that could be sold for a nice profit here in Polpo. This place is so remote and the Lohtang Pass is snowed up and impassable for so much of the year that goods from outside like flashlights, radios, batteries, and sugar are hard to get hold of. In return, the Polpo villages trade Chinese goods they've bought over the border in Tibet. They sell cloth, jewelry . . . even sheep. Yes! Your porter, Ang, is now the proud owner of four sheep traded for a portable stereo he's somehow brought along with all the other things he had to carry. Traditionally, the trade between the high barren valleys and the foothills was salt in exchange for grain. Caravans of hundreds of yaks loaded with salt from Tibet were taken down trails like the ones you have walked thus far. On the return trip, the yaks would bring back grain like corn, which is hard to grow in the high, dry valleys. This trade is dying out now that roads have been built, so getting hold of salt is no longer a problem on the lowland side of the mountains.

There are still yaks here, though, and Da-Lhamhu thinks you could get a good deal on hiring one to carry the climbing gear and remaining food on the next leg of the journey.

Yak facts

- Yaks are big, wild cows. They're related to the aurochs — the oxen that used to roam the European forests in cavemen times.
- The shaggy hair along their sides often reaches down to the ground. It becomes matted and makes a good insulating layer between the yak and the snow when the yak lies down.
- Wild yaks are larger and blacker than domestic yaks, which are often brown or spotted black-and-white.
- Yak butter tea (tea with butter added instead of milk) is a popular drink in the Himalayas.
- Yak dung is fantastic as fuel!
- There are very few wild yaks left.
- Yaks can only survive in the cold at high altitudes. In fact, they often die when they are taken to the hot lowlands.
- Their coarse, long hair is useful for making ropes, while the silky under-hair can be woven into fine cloth.
- If you breed a yak with a cow you get a zo. These are smaller than yaks. Some are spotted and many don't have horns.

Pack yaks or human porters? — Quiz

So what's it going to be? Pack yaks or human porters to lug the stuff? Look at the list below and work out which sentences go with yaks and which ones go with Polpo porters.

a) Can find food along the way.
b) Need to carry all their own food.
c) Can walk along narrow cliff-edge trails.
d) Cannot manage the steepest slopes.
e) Can carry three- or four-man loads.
f) May refuse to go on if the going gets too tough.
g) Need to have a "driver."
h) Not available at every village, just ones where ethnic Tibetans live.
i) May not be available at certain times of year, such as harvest time.

Answers on next page

Consider the situation. The next stage to Thamap is easy with no cliff-edge trails. There are yaks here for hire — at a good price. Da-Lhamhu says that this time you should go with yaks. In fact, she knows just the man to help you — a distant cousin called Tilen Thundup. He has two yaks, Milli and Mooni. Here he is with one of them.

A day of rest follows and then you're off on your way again — you, Da-Lhamhu, Tilen Thundup, and the two yaks. Ahead of you, gleaming white in the sunlight, is "Dangiroba." Next stop, the monastery at the foot of the mountain. Thamap!

Answers from page 57

Human Porters: b, c, f, i.
Pack yaks: a, d, e, g, h.

Chapter 7

THE GREAT GAME, BUTTER TEA AND SNOW-ICE

From Polpo, it's a two-day trek to the foot of the mountain. The uphill track is dry and dusty. You begin to wish you could've stayed at the same level as the Lohtang Pass rather than descending to Polpo, because now you've got to regain all that height, and then climb even higher. That isn't easy in the thin air. Still, with Tilen Thundup's two yaks carrying all your gear, at least you don't feel laden down like you did on the first part of your trek.

In the nineteenth century, many "Tibetan" areas, like Polpo, were forbidden territory. Wedged between India and central Asia (the British and Russian empires), Tibet and the kingdoms around its edges were wary about outsiders entering their borders. Great Britain and Russia were always looking for ways to increase their territory. They sent agents on scouting missions all over the Himalayas. They called this the "Great Game." Most of the British agents were Indians from the foothills who traveled disguised as traders or holy men. They were called "pundits" (teachers) and were told to make very careful notes about what they saw and take measurements of the distances they walked so that accurate maps could be made later. These were perilous missions as the pundits risked death if they were caught.

Pundit tricks

These are some of the pundits' tricks of the trade and some of the things that happened to them...

- Pundits were taught to walk exactly 2,000 paces to the mile and to keep track of the distances traveled on specially altered sets of prayer beads. One pundit who was traveling with a trade caravan that was galloping through bandit-ridden territory had to count horse steps instead for 230 miles (370 km).

- Some pundits carried Buddhist prayer wheels, in which they kept maps and notes instead of prayers. Pundit Nain Singh found that he could keep fellow travelers from coming too close by whirling the wheel and pretending to pray.

- Detained by a Tibetan border official, Pundit Hari Ram was asked to cure the man's sick wife. He looked in his medical book and gave her some pills. Luckily for him she got better and Hari Ram was allowed to continue. At one stage of his journey, he came to a river that flowed through a chasm hundreds of meters deep. The path he had to walk to the bridge that crossed it was made of iron bars and stone slabs jutting out of the cliff-edge. The path was never more than fifty centimeters wide and in places it was half that width! Hari Ram had to walk half a kilometer along it. On his journey, he traveled all the way around Mount Everest though he never actually saw it because there were other mountains in the way.

An easy two-day journey brings you to Thamap. The *Gompa* (Buddhist monastery) is set on a narrow ridge overlooking the valley you've been trekking through from Polpo. Prayer flags line the way up the ridge path to the metal-studded door. You knock, and while you wait for someone to open the door you idly spin one of the red-and-gold prayer wheels that are set into alcoves in the wall on either side of the entrance. You have come to show your respect for the Lama of the monastery before you set off to "Dangiroba." Da-Lhamhu says that few outsiders come here and that it is only right to ask the holy man's permission before you proceed with your adventure.

The door creaks open and a young shaven-headed nun in maroon robes shows you in. She gestures for you to remove your hiking boots. In the next room, it is smoky and pungent with burning incense. By the flickering light of what looks like butter burning in dishes, you make out several cross-legged monks sitting against the walls. Behind them are paintings and

ancient-looking statues of the Buddha set in recesses in the walls. The monks are chanting monotonous mantras, "Om Padi Mani Hum," from long leather-bound prayer sheets. The effect of their mumbling and the thick, scented air is slightly hypnotic. At the end of the hall sits an important-looking man in thick, square glasses. He is a lama, a holy man. Many years back, after the previous lama died, monks were sent out to search for a boy born at that time who seemed to have wisdom "beyond his years." The old lama had described where he might be found. This holy man bidding you to sit in front of him is that boy now grown up.

The nun who showed you in reappears. She is holding a thermos flask from which she pours a thick, steaming, yellowy-brown liquid. Yak butter tea! You have to drink it since it would be rude not to. Better to do this in one gulp. It's like hot butter with just a hint of tea. "You like it?" The nun offers you more. What can you do but down another cupful, smiling as politely as you can, while Da-Lhamhu talks earnestly to the holy man, who turns to you, says some words you don't understand, and nods his head. You have his blessing to climb "Dangiroba."

You will set off in two days. That will give you a little more time to acclimatize to the altitude. Da-Lhamhu will go and hire a couple of men from the farmhouses near Thamap to help carry your equipment part of the way up the mountain in preparation for your attempt at the summit. Tilen Thundup will come to your base camp, too, but he will have to leave his two yaks out to graze on the mountain's scrubby lower slopes. The path ahead is too difficult for them. The time has finally come to open those two knapsacks of specialized climbing gear. In the courtyard of Thamap Gompa, you spread out the gear and familiarize yourself with what each piece is used for.

Mountain gear quiz — part 1

What does each piece of equipment do?

1. Jumar	A. Anchors you as you slide down the mountainside on your way to certain oblivion.
2. Harness	B. Keeps your toes in to spike your way up those tricky ice walls.
3. Ice ax	C. Tells you how high you've climbed up the mountain.
4. Altimeter	D. Lets you breathe freely when the air around you has become too thin to give you the oxygen you need.
5. Oxygen tanks and mask	E. Ropes you to a safety line ... or to your sherpa, for that matter.
6. Crampons	F. Helps you climb up ropes.

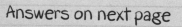

Answers on next page

Answers from page 65

1. F — You can slide it up the rope but it locks still when you try to move it down.
2. E — The harness provides a safe point to rope yourself onto. You can clip yourself on and off using a carabiner clip, or "crab."
3. A — You'll need two to claw your way up. Good for hacking a grip into the ice and rock, for cutting ice-steps, and . . . serving as an anchor if you slip.
4. C — If you had a Global Positioning System (GPS), that would also tell you how high you are above sea level if it could lock onto four satellite signals. Needed for climbing the very highest mountains.
5. D — You could climb "Dangiroba" without using these. They're really just a backup if you suffer health problems caused by altitude. Other items that will come into use here are snow goggles, a climbing helmet, thermal insulating inner layers, and a waterproof/windproof, breathable outer shell.
6. B — These are best fixed to those plastic, lined mountain boots you've been carrying all the way.

Mountain gear Quiz — part 2

Gripping rock and ice

These are some pieces of equipment designed for attaching your rope to the mountain.
One can be attached to **solid ice**, one hammers into less firm "**snow-ice**," and the other wedges into cracks in **rock** . . .

"Deadman"
"bolt"
"ice screw"

Which piece of gear is attached to which of these surfaces?

Answers on page 69

A half-day's climb from Thamap brings you to the snow line. First there are just patches of snow in places where the sun rarely reaches. Further up, the snow cover is more or less continuous, but for the most part, it's wet and slushy. The fierce sunshine has melted the upper layer, which sits soggily on top of compacted snow-ice. This is snow that's melted and frozen many times. It's not as hard as true ice, but it isn't soft like freshly fallen snow either. You put on your dark snow goggles to protect your eyes from the glare of all that whiteness and continue on up.

At a rest stop, you lift your goggles and look ahead. The sunlight up here is dazzling for sure, but that snow over there looks pink! Is this some weird optical illusion? Have your eyes not adjusted to the sudden brightness?
No. The pink blush to the snow is because of microscopic plants, called algae, that live under the surface. They absorb the tiny trace of nutrients in the snow and use sunlight to make food for themselves by photosynthesis. The reason why these plants look red and not green is because of a red pigment that protects them from the full glare of the sunlight — a bit like sunglasses.

There is other life here too — splotches of lichen on some of the bare rocks. They grow so slowly that a blotch more than a few centimeters across may have taken hundreds of years to grow. Around the rocks and under the snow there are also tiny spiders, insects, and centipedes. They have special antifreeze chemicals in their bodies to survive in the intense cold. They live on microorganisms in the dust that gets blown up here from the lowlands. As for bigger animals, there is no sign . . . BUT . . . something speeds off, just on the edge of your vision. Not a yeti — a Tibetan snowcock. What does it live on up here? Basically, whatever pieces of plants it can find.

Answers from page 67

Deadman and **snow-ice** — hammer it in with your ice ax.
Bolt and **rock** — this is usually the most secure of the three methods.
Ice screw and **solid ice** — screw it in with the handle of your ice ax.

There's also an extendable, lightweight aluminum ladder that Tilen Thundup acquired from a previous climbing expedition that came to the area. What on Earth is that for? (The answer is in Chapter 9.)

Soon the snow is continuous, except for a few rocky outcrops that protrude from the white blanket. You strap the crampons onto the soles of your boots for a better grip. With each step you crunch against the icy crust that has frozen on top of the snow in the night, then sink thigh-deep into the mush underneath. It's easier to let Da-Lhamhu lead for a while with you following in her tracks.

You're really feeling the altitude again. Although you acclimatized in the foothills at Darpeeling, then again at Thamap, the air up here is so thin that you find you have to rest every few steps and catch your breath. Each time you stop, you can hear your pulse pounding around your brain, feel your head aching, and, if you move too quickly, you start feeling dizzy.

With temperatures that can drop to minus forty, howling, icy winds, and a lack of oxygen to breathe, you're in an environment that your body isn't designed for. To climb "Dangiroba" you'll be working against your physical limits. Will you make it? Will you survive?

Chapter 8
THE PERILOUS SNOWFIELDS

The freezing high snowfields. This is what can happen to your body up here...

A. Snow blindness — caused by the dazzling light and tiny ice particles blowing across your eyes. It feels as though grit has been scraped across them. You weep continuously. It's painful with your eyes closed, and doubly so if you try to open them.

B. Frostbite — fingers and toes can freeze hard. The tissue dies and has to be cut off or else gangrene will set in and kill you. French climber Maurice Herzog was climbing down Annapurna in 1950 when he accidentally dropped his gloves while searching in his knapsack for some condensed milk and his barometer-altimeter. He clambered down to his camp, gripping the rocks and snow with his bare hands. By the time he arrived, his fingers were blotched "violet and white and

[were] as hard as wood." Most of them had to be amputated. When Eric Shipton, a British climber, had a frostbitten foot, his guide soothed it with a poultice made of cheese mixed with ash from his yak-dung fire and his foot was saved.

C. Hypothermia – this is when your body gets chilled. You lose coordination and eventually consciousness. If you're not warmed up, you die.

D. Sunburn – all that white snow reflects the sunlight so well.

E. Dehydration – your body loses liquid when you are climbing, through sweat and through the moisture in the air you breathe out. As your blood has more red cells it is thicker and you can have blood clots. These are incredibly painful and potentially fatal if one happens in your brain.

F. Cerebral edema – fluid leaks into your brain, causing it to swell and squash against the inside of your skull. You have incredibly bad headaches and feel drowsy and unsteady. You may also lose consciousness and die.

G. Pulmonary edema – this time the fluid leaks into your lungs and you become breathless and choke on frothy fluid.

Added to that, there's the problem of retinal hemorrhages when blood vessels burst at the back of your eye, causing blurred vision and sometimes blindness. And just when you need extra energy for all that climbing, you lose your appetite. The mere thought of food makes you feel sick.

Now let's see if you can figure out what the treatments for the climbing ailments are.

For both cerebral and pulmonary edema, the thing to do is to lose altitude fast. Even a drop of a few hundred meters will probably cure you. As for the other problems, you have to work them out for yourself. Here is the choice of treatments ... Match the number to the letter of the ailment on the previous pages.

2. Goggles/sunglasses with sidepieces.

1. Sunblock cream.

3. Wear insulating gloves and socks and check fingers and toes when possible.

4. Drink five or six liters of water each day.

5. Wear warm clothing.

Answers on page 75

Don't worry. That headache you've got and the blood-pounding sensation is just mild altitude sickness. It is unpleasant but it should ease off as you acclimatize, provided that you keep drinking lots of water.

Ahead of you, Da-Lhamhu has stopped by a flat area of snow, sheltered partly from the wind by an outcrop of rocks. Above it rises the rock face of "Dangiroba." This, she announces, will be your base camp for the final ascent of the mountain. Presently, Tilen Thundup and the two Thamap porters arrive. After depositing your equipment they will return to the monastery. "Good luck," Tilen Thundup says — and don't worry about your supplies for the return journey. They will be safe at Thamap.

It is late afternoon. After putting up your tent, you and Da-Lhamhu must look at the mountain and decide on a route to take. There are various things you will have to consider.

Match the thing to consider with the reason why ...

Things to consider	Reason why
1. Fresh snow on steep slopes.	A. It may be windy and progress may be slow with sections of rock climbing, but at least there is no avalanche risk.
2. Crossing snowfields in the early morning.	B. This could easily slip and cause an avalanche.
3. Walking the ridges.	C. The second person wastes less energy.
4. Walking one person behind the other through deep snow and swapping places.	D. The upper snow crust is still frozen hard, so you don't break through and waste energy ploughing through deep snow.

Answers on page 79

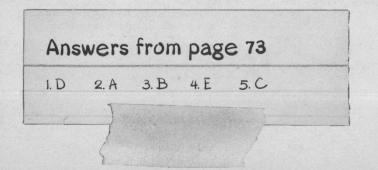

Answers from page 73

1. D   2. A   3. B   4. E   5. C

Avalanche!

Avalanches are one of the major risks. In 1922, on a British expedition to climb Mount Everest, nine sherpas were swept over an ice-cliff by an avalanche. Fresh snow had fallen during the night and George Leigh Mallory, the climber leading the men, had continued ahead in the warm afternoon sunshine rather than losing time by looking for other possible routes. Mallory, himself, and three men roped together with him were also swept along with the snowslide. Luckily, they were near the edge of it, caught in the newly fallen softer snow rather than in the main part of the fall where heavy ice blocks would have crushed them. The four men dug themselves out quickly and then managed to save two of the sherpas behind them. The other seven died, as did Mallory himself, on a subsequent attempt on Everest two years later. His body was found by climbers on the mountain in 1999. The other climber with him, George Irving, was never found and people still wonder whether Mallory and Irving, not Edmund Hillary and Sherpa Tensing Norgay, were actually the first to climb the highest mountain in the world.

If you do get caught in an avalanche, here's what to do ...

1. You can't outrun an avalanche. If you do get caught, try to swim up as best you can and, if at all possible, stay on top of the snow.

2. When the snow stops moving, try to scrabble up and out. You may be buried in snow and disoriented, so "up" may be hard to find. Spit and see which way it drops, then try to move the opposite way before you suffocate.

3. If you're roped onto someone it might be easier for people to find you. Off-piste skiers (those who ski off the trail of compacted snow) often carry special radio alarms that give out a signal for rescuers to find them. Unfortunately, this will not be an option on your expedition, as you have no backup.

Without backup to support you, you're going to have to take things very carefully. When climbers have set out to climb the biggest Himalayan mountains like Everest and K2, they have generally gone about it in one of two ways:

1. What they call "siege tactics." They get a huge team together with relays of sherpas and porters ferrying supplies up to higher and higher camps just to support a few climbers who will actually make the "assault" on the summit. This was how the first successful Everest expedition in 1953 was done. Siege — tactics expeditions are huge, expensive, and complicated, but safer for the climbers than ...

2. "Alpine-style climbing." A small team tackles the whole mountain together, carrying all the equipment needed. Some, "like British climber Alison Hargreaves in 1995," have tackled Everest "solo" (alone); she did this without even carrying extra oxygen to breathe.

"Alpine climbing" is obviously riskier. There are times when you have to assess the danger to yourself and your party. Climbing this peak is not worth your life or your guide's life. There are far too many stories of mountaineers who didn't make it.

From your base camp, these are the routes that you could climb up "Dangiroba." Da-Lhamhu chooses the safest route. Decide which route that is, but remember . . . all have risks.

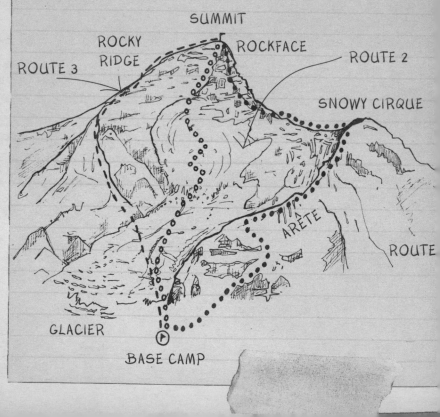

SUMMIT

ROCKY RIDGE

ROCKFACE

ROUTE 3

ROUTE 2

SNOWY CIRQUE

ARETE

ROUTE

GLACIER

BASE CAMP

1. Walk along the arête, then climb the rock face (a technical climb needing ropes). An arête is a very narrow ridge that has been carved out on both sides by glaciers scooping away the mountain. There are cliff edges on both sides and the way you would have to walk would be along the rocky top edge.

2. Climb the snowy cirque. A cirque or corrie is a hollowed-out "bowl" with very steep edges. This cirque is covered in snow and faces south so that, weather permitting, sunlight falls directly on it for much of the day.

3. Cross the glacier and then ascend the rocky ridge. The glacier is a very slow-moving river of snow. As it moves, it scours away the mountain below it. The glacier travels too slowly for you to sense any movement, but dangerous cracks called crevasses may open up.

Which route would you choose?

Answers on page 80

Answers from page 75

1. B   2. D   3. A   4. C

Answers from page 79

1. This route is too dangerous because the high winds may blow yo[u] off the ridge, and the rock face is almost certainly too difficult t[o] attempt in the freezing and windy conditions you would face.

2. The snow will melt slightly in the sunlight, which is a severe avalanche risk, especially later in the day.

3. This is Da-Lhamhu's choice as it imposes the least risk.

Here's why . . . This route is risky, because some crevasses might be hidden by snow covering the glacier. You might fall down them. But if you proceed carefully, once you've crossed the glacier, the rest of the ascent should be relatively straightforward. There is just one drawback. This slow and steady method of climbing "Dangiroba'" makes sense but, unless conditions are near perfect, you may end up sleeping out on the mountain. So take your sleeping gear and be prepared to rope yourself to a ledge . . .

It's a long night for you and it's very cold, despite the fact that you're wearing most of your cold-weather clothing inside your sleeping bag. You sleep badly, possibly one of the effects of altitude, and possibly because of your anxiety about tomorrow's climb. This is the final test. Will you make it up "Dangiroba" or will the difficult climb prove too much?

Chapter 9
TO THE SUMMIT...
AND BEYOND!

Just before dawn, Da-Lhamhu nudges you and tells you that it's time to get ready. You put on your boots, strap on your crampons, and check that you have everything you need. You shouldn't need the oxygen mask and cylinder but you take it anyway, just to help you out if you need it.

Trudging along some tracks that Da-Lhamhu must have made yesterday, you soon reach the glacier. It's a river of ice flowing down the steep mountainside fifty centimeters to a meter a day. The surface is steep, uneven, and in places dotted with rocks which at some time have fallen from the cliff-faces that loom above the glacier's sides. You've only been going for twenty minutes and already you're straining for breath at this height. Da-Lhamhu slowly leads the way, probing the snow ahead of her to check that there is a firm footing. Snowfall could have covered a crack in the ice – a crevasse. If you trod there, who knows how far you'd fall.

Maybe you'd be lucky like Austrian Reinhold Messner was when he fell down a crevasse while climbing Mount Everest in 1980.

There was no warning. The snow beneath his feet just gave way and he fell, coming to an abrupt halt an instant later. Turning on his head torch, Messner surveyed the situation and fought back the panic. The ice crack continued down as far as he could see in the torch beam. Eight meters above, he could see the hole in the snow where he had fallen. By some amazing fluke he had landed on a narrow bridge of transparent ice roughly one meter square that spanned the crevasse, but now he was stuck. The blue-green ice walls narrowed above him with overhangs that looked impossible to climb. Luckily, he kept calm. He spotted a slanted snow-covered ledge nearby, which he carefully reached out for, and he transferred his weight across. The ledge held and slowly he inched his way back up to freedom and continued his climb. That day he became the first person to reach the summit solo.

Da-Lhamhu says that you have to look the glacier over and work out where the crevasses might be. They often occur where the ice flows suddenly down a steeper slope, but they might be so covered with snow-ice that's built up at the edges and snow that's fallen that you you have to look for faint lines in the snow-field to work out where they are. Sometimes the snow bridges that have formed over crevasses are strong enough to hold a person's weight. But sometimes they're not!

Crossing the crevasses: Quiz

In the following questions, each of these pieces of equipment is used ONCE except for the ice ax, which is used twice ...

- Ice ax
- Snow ladder
- Ice screw
- Jumar
- Crampons
- Harness

You might want to look back to the mountain gear quiz in Chapter 7 to see what they each do.

Da-Lhamhu slowly leads the way. You're roped together, separated by about six meters of rope that you try to keep fairly taut so that you can quickly react to any sudden jerk if your partner falls.

1. Which part of your gear should you
    fix the rope to?

(Note: you each keep several
meters of rope free at the ends.
You wrap it around yourselves
just in case you need to res-
cue your partner. Also, you
have a loop tied in the rope
close to you.)

2. Which piece of equipment
    should you hold to anchor you
    and your partner in case of a
    fall? (The rope, not you, will then
    take the strain.)

You slowly zigzag up the glacier,
crossing the cracks at the ends
where they close together and
occasionally trying out the
snow bridges that cross some
of the crevasses.

The crevasses you find at first are just cracks in the glacier ice that you can step across. But when you reach a gap three meters wide, it looks like you're in for serious delays. But Da-Lhamhu just smiles and says "no problem."

3. What piece of gear should you use to bridge the gap?

After you've crossed the crevasse, you continue upwards, leaving your bridge in place for your return. The next crevasse is far too broad to use the ladder though it is only ten meters deep. You could use a rope to rappel down and then clamber around the jagged seracs (ice pillars) before climbing up the other side. You need to attach a rope to the hard ice at the top. Look back at your mountain gear list.

4. Which piece of gear can you use to attach the rope to the ice?

You rappel (lower yourself) down and carefully pick your way between the blocks of ice that have fallen from the far side of the crevasse.
Now you'll have to climb up the sheer ice face on the other side.

5. What can you hold in your hands to grip the ice as you climb?
6. What piece of gear (attached to boots) do you kick into the ice wall to get a grip?

You slowly climb the crevasse wall, attaching snow screws to clip your rope to. If you lose your grip, you'll only fall a short way. It's tiring work, but eventually you get to the top where you attach another rope, which Da-Lhamhu can climb up.

7. Which piece of equipment lets your sherpa climb up the rope?

Answers on page 88

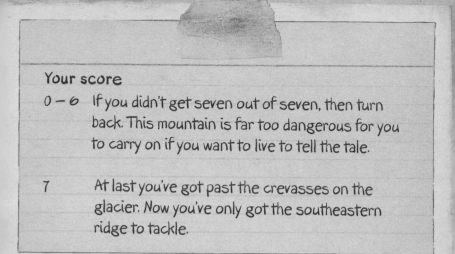

Your score

0 — 6	If you didn't get seven out of seven, then turn back. This mountain is far too dangerous for you to carry on if you want to live to tell the tale.
7	At last you've got past the crevasses on the glacier. Now you've only got the southeastern ridge to tackle.

You and Da-Lhamhu pause to drink some water. Climbing out of that crevasse was hot work, and you must replace valuable liquid lost by sweating. You look at your watch. It's nearly ten o'clock. You haven't lost too much time on the glacier, so you decide to continue with the climb. You should just be able to reach the summit and return at daylight!

If you did not score seven out of seven on the crevasses quiz, and you took longer — say thirty minutes — for each wrong answer, what time would you have arrived at this point? More than an hour late, and you might have to consider returning to your base camp. You would not have enough time to reach the summit and return within the hours of daylight. You could leave the ice screws, ropes, and ladder in place for a second attempt at the summit tomorrow. Alternatively, you could move your tent and food supplies to a higher point above the glacier and start out from that place tomorrow morning.

Answers from pages 83-86

1. Harness
2. Ice ax
3. Snow ladder
4. Ice screw
5. Ice ax
6. Crampons
7. Jumar

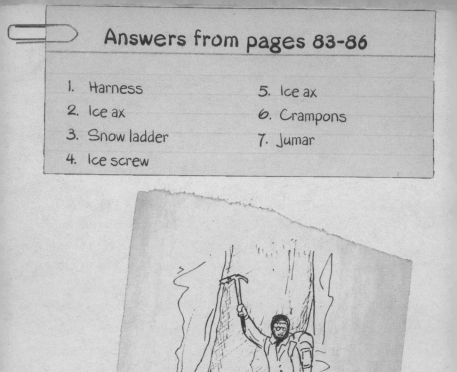

"CHIMNEYING UP"

Tackling the southeastern ridge...

The ridge seems to go on forever. There is only a fine dusting of snow here and you're walking — and in places climbing — bare rock and patches of ice. On one rocky outcrop where the edge abruptly "steps" up, you have to chimney up, pressing your feet against an ice wall on one side and a cliff on the other, and maneuvering yourself up bit by bit.

Surprisingly, there is little wind up here today, though you can see by the sculpted ice "cornices" on the ridge edges that at times it must be very strong indeed. You can see clouds below you. It feels as if you are above the weather. You climb in dazzling sunlight, clambering up each knob of rock thinking this is the last one, only to be faced with more of the same ahead. You feel you're going on willpower alone now. How much easier it would be to stop and turn back! The air is so thin that every few steps you have to stop and catch your breath. Every hour or so you allow yourself a longer rest. You haven't needed the extra oxygen yet. You've decided to save that for when the situation becomes desperate.

You continue upwards, all thoughts out of your mind except "Go forward" until, suddenly, there is no more up. You're on the summit! Everything else is below you. It takes a minute or two for that to sink in. You've made it! You and Da-Lhamhu are the first people ever to reach the summit of "Dangiroba." You'll be famous when you get back. The international media will

ICE CORNICE

want to know your story. Your climbing friends will be envious and want to know how you achieved this "first." Da-Lhamhu will have no trouble finding expeditions to guide with a Himalayan "first ascent" to her name. Perhaps you two should go into business and start your own trekking agency.

You find the small flag you brought for this moment and wedge it upright as best you can between some rocks. Then you set your camera to timing mode, place it on your knapsack, and pose with your guide for some photographs. Then you look at the view . . .

It's as if you're on top of the world — truly breathtaking. You can see other high white Himalayas in the distance and, if you look carefully, you should be able to see the way you've come.

- Darpeeling, where you acclimatized to the altitude.
- Nali, where you hired your porters.
- Your trek through the forest and . . .
- Over the Lohtang Pass . . . to Polpo.
- The Gompa (monastery) at Thamap, then up to . . .
- Your base camp.
- The glacier with its many crevasses, and then the southeastern ridge.

Work out the way you came. Which hexagons did you climb through?

92

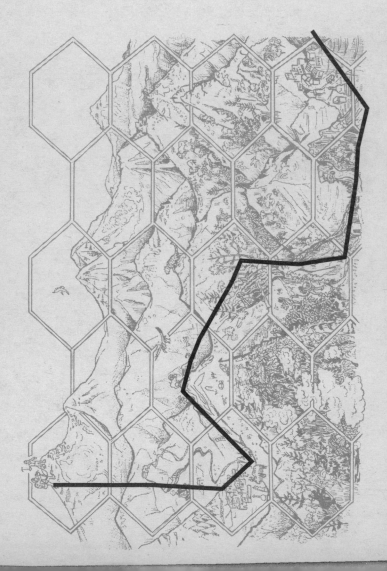

Da-Lhamhu brings you "back down to Earth." She points to your watch. It's time to leave the summit if you're going to get back down to base camp before darkness falls. Unlike Marco Siffredi, who snowboarded down Everest, or Jean-Marc Boivin, who paraglided from the summit, you are going to have to walk. And on those icy rocks, despite your tiredness, there is little room for error. At least on some of the snow bits you can glissade down (a climber's term for sliding), and when you get to base camp you can think of some of the other adventures you could have — like exploring **South Sea Islands** or trekking through the parched vastness of the **Sahara Desert**. Perhaps you've decided you like snow and cold so much you'll opt for the **Arctic**. Whichever one,

EXPLORERS WANTED!

Your mission...

should you choose to accept it,
is to journey through the blazing Sahara
in search of a lost waterfall!

Are you ready for the challenge?

Explorers Wanted to:

- Journey across endless sand dunes
- Battle thirst, mirages, and heatstroke
- Care for and ride their very own camel
- Survive brushes with scorpions and vipers
- Meet the people of the veil

Includes the author's own expedition notes and sketches!

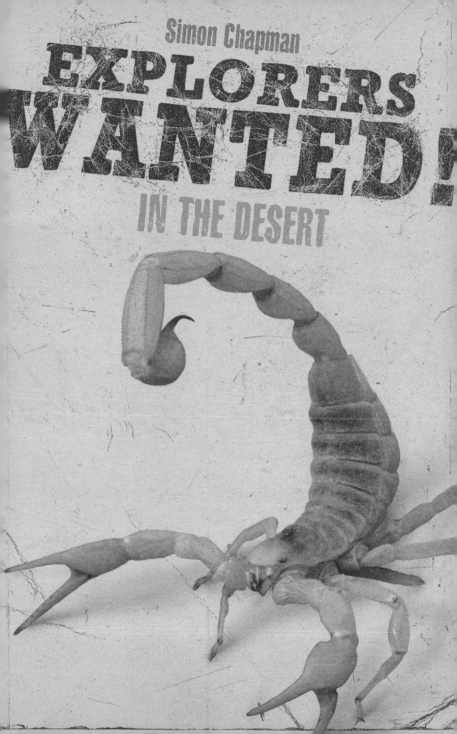

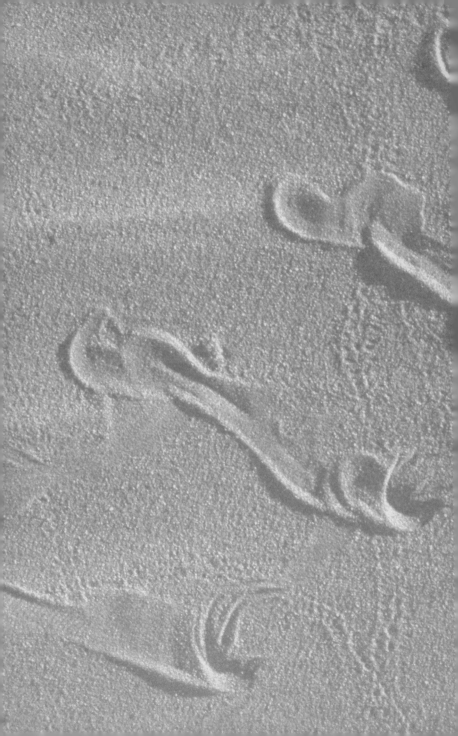

SO ... YOU WANT TO EXPLORE THE SAHARA DESERT?

You want to ...

traverse the endless **dunes** by camel?

drink your fill in a **sparkling oasis?**

encounter the **exotic people** and **strange creatures** that inhabit this arid wasteland ?

If the answer to any of these questions is YES, then

this is the book for you, so read on ...

THIS BOOK GIVES YOU the essential lowdown on life in this land of extremes, from how to cope with the intense heat and burning sun to **where you might find water** when at first glance there appears to be none. There'll also be the stories of some of the people who came before you, how they survived (or didn't!) in this, the greatest desert on Earth.

YOUR MISSION ... should you choose

to accept it, is to get to the Ahaggan massif. Beyond the miles of flat gravel pans, the rocky *hammada*, and the great sand sea of Najmer stands a huge slab of rock, sculpted over the centuries by wind-blown sand into fantastic pinnacles and deep gorges, which the sun's rays never reach. The Tuareg camel caravans of the deep desert have avoided the Ahaggan over the years. There was no water or food for their animals. It was too easy to lose yourself in the treacherous terrain. Until recently, that is. . . . Forced to shelter in the rocks by a sudden sand-storm, a group of nomads, separated from their caravan, made a startling discovery. WATER. Cool and fresh and lots of it. When they finally made it out of the sand sea and *hammada* rock fields, the men told stories of a lost canyon with a lake and even a waterfall. Painted on the anyon's walls were figures of giraffes, hippos, and ebras, animals of the African plains, not the Sahara desert. Seeing the state the men were in when they were found, few believed their story, especially since they could not explain how to get back to the valley.

So what is the truth? Could there really be a waterfall in the desert? What about the rock paintings? Who drew them and when? This is what you've set yourself to find out. Getting there will be some adventure. Just how will you start?

DJELLA OASIS

WELL AT BILAN

SAND SEA OF NAJMER

AHAGGAN MASSIF

Time to set the scene...

The Sahara desert is HUGE...

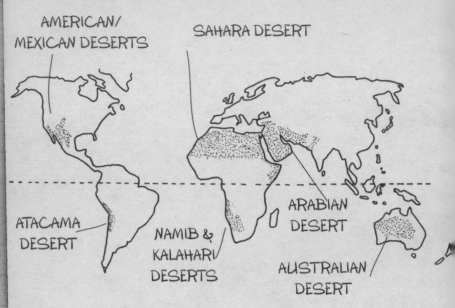

AMERICAN/
MEXICAN DESERTS

SAHARA DESERT

ATACAMA
DESERT

NAMIB &
KALAHARI
DESERTS

ARABIAN
DESERT

AUSTRALIAN
DESERT

It stretches right across the top of Africa and other deserts
carry on beyond that through Arabia, the Middle East, and as far
as southern Pakistan and western India. Here it is hot, dry, and
parched. The ground is rocky or sandy, in some places dotted
with hardy plants that can endure the intense heat and lack of
water, in other places totally barren. The Sahara and Middle
East aren't the only hot deserts. If you look at a map of the world
you'll notice other deserts, like the Namib and the Kalahari,
mirrored across the equator in southern Africa. And if you
look at North and South America you'll notice the same thing,
desert in both north and south, jungle in between.

It's all to do with the way the sun heats the Earth. At the equator, hot air rises (it's called convection). Moist air from the oceans rushes in, so everything's wet and jungly. The air — no moisture in it — falls at the Tropics of Cancer and

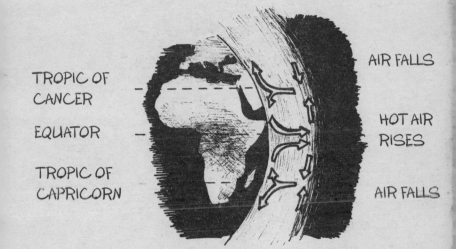

TROPIC OF
CANCER

EQUATOR

TROPIC OF
CAPRICORN

AIR FALLS

HOT AIR
RISES

AIR FALLS

Capricorn. Those areas are deserts. Generally the winds blow away from there, taking away any moisture. So it's mostly cloudless, hot, and incredibly dry. But are all deserts the same?

Certainly many desert animals across the world have developed similar adaptations ...

About the author

Writer and broadcaster Simon Chapman is a self-confessed jungle addict, making expeditions whenever he can. His travels have taken him to tropical forests all over the world, from Borneo and Irian Jaya to the Amazon.

The story of his search for a mythical Giant Ape in the Bolivian rainforest, *The Monster of the Madidi*, was published in 2001. He has also had numerous articles and illustrations published in magazines in Britain and the United States, including *Wanderlust*, *BBC Wildlife*, and *South American Explorer*. He has written and recorded for BBC Radio 4 and lectured on the organization of jungle expeditions at the Royal Geographical Society, of which he is a fellow. When not exploring, Simon lives with his wife and his two young children in Lancaster, England, where he teaches high school physics.